RESILIENT SAILING

10 Lessons to Persevere in Life's Stormy Seas

DR. CARL M. BARNES

CDR, USN, (Ret.)

Resilient Sailing

10 Lessons To Persevere in Life's Stormy Seas

By: Dr. Carl M. Barnes

Trient Press

3375 S Rainbow Blvd

#81710, SMB 13135

Las Vegas,NV 89180

Ordering Information:

Quantity sales. Special discounts are available on quantity purchases by corporations, associations, and others. For details, contact the publisher at the address above.

Orders by U.S. trade bookstores and wholesalers. Please contact Trient Press: Tel: (775) 996-3844;   or visit www.trientpress.com.

Printed in the United States of America

Publisher's Cataloging-in-Publication data

Barnes, Dr. Carl M.

A title of a book : Resilient Sailing

ISBN

      Paperback : 978-1-955198-28-8

      E-book   : 978-1-955198-29-5

"I want to thank you for your 35 years of service"

-Jack Canfield

Forward by:
Antonio T. Smith, Jr.

Resilient Sailing is one of the most touching and encouraging pieces of work that I've read in a very longtime. It is often hard to find your bearings in rough seas. For many know all too well, billows may roll and breakers may dash, but when you are anchored to something much stronger than the storms of life, you always end up sailing where you wanted to go.

Carl, such as myself had a tough life…really tough. We share the same feelings of abandonment, betrayal, and loneliness during our tender years; years in which we should have been sheltered and loved beyond measure. Yet, life did not deal us cotton candy, life dealt us medicine in candy wrappers.

"My pain was the type that morphine could not cure" –Carl M. Barnes, CDR USN (Retired), embodies one of my favorite reminders about Carl. If anyone knows how to be resilient, it is him. Carl is no stranger to the "downs" of life. This is why he has been called by God, himself, to remind us all that focusing on the bad times and our failures, is not in the Will of God for us.

I think my favorite part in *Resilient Sailing* is, "As a Chaplain, I relied on listening to voices that belong to prominent people above and below in the chain of command to guide Sailors in the right direction, be it metaphysically or in their careers. And in doing so, I learned that the measure of a man's character is the voice he chooses to listen to." I find great comfort in knowing that I have a friend in Carl, one who can be both practical and metaphysical, while remaining empathetic to me at all times. Anyone who knows Carl knows he does this very well. Carl is a gift to mankind and I am grateful to know him and to write about his book and character to you, dear reader.

The truth is, this world needs more Carls. We all need a friend who can be our Chaplain and our psychologist. Kindness is so rare these days, we often feel people have a hidden agenda when they are kind to us. Not Carl. He is always kind and patient, and never expects anything in return.

I don't know what you are up against and I don't know what you are facing. But here's what I know about you without even knowing you. You can plant better seeds to get a better life, and you can dominate the demands of this reality. I know that everything is perfect and *Resilient Sailing* is your divine reminder of God's sovereignty in your life and His power within you.

If you fell down yesterday, remember you are a Resilient Sailor, conquering all the waves of life.

P.S. I am so proud of Carl. He has become my friend, my coach, and spiritual mentor.

~Antonio T Smith Jr

Letter from Cozy Corner

Dr. Carl M. Barnes is definitely someone special to the Cozy Corner Family. He has been an intricate roll in the growth of Cozy Corner Publishing and without him, there wouldn't be certain processes and procedures in place.

We have truly enjoyed working with Dr. Barnes. He is truly a man of honor and he lives what he speaks. We hope you learn just as much from this wonderful work as we did from the author himself. We encourage you to take the nuggets given in this work and apply them to your life as we have seen the product of resiliency through Dr. Barnes.

Thank you, Dr Barnes, for choosing Cozy Corner. It has been a two way blessing.

Deaunna M. Mitchell
CEO, Cozy Corner Publishing

Table of Contents

"With an Attitude of Gratitude"

~Dr. Carl M. Barnes~

The Introduction

Someone said that life is like an onion, you must peel it one layer at a time. And sometimes you cry. Most people who have experienced peeling onions know that it has a way of producing crocodile tears. Yes, you cry.

Based on my decades of in the trenches experience of overcoming insurmountable odds and rejections, I want to share my lessons learned with you. So, if you've ever suffered
setbacks, hopelessness, confused, betrayed, running against a brick wall, then know YOU are not alone on this journey to your PROMISED LAND.

Each time I felt depressed, I would draw upon the lessons learned that PUSHED me to NOT GIVE UP.

No matter where you are in life, and regardless of how old or young you are, you can be Resilient. This book will help you make the necessary adjustments in your life so you can know that there are HIDDEN treasures within YOU. By reading this book, and applying these lessons you will:

***Understand What Crazy Faith Is
***Development an Attitude of Gratitude
***Face your Darkness
***Ask for help

By the time you finish this book, you will be able to say, "I can face Life's Stormy Seas!" You will be able to see not just what is, but also what can be, so that you can be more resilient than ever.

~Dr. Carl M Barnes

The Foundation

I was born into the life of a very loving, yet, confused 17-year old African American women and an 18-year old African American high school jock, both residing in Wilson, North Carolina. But, before I was even born, I almost became a real statistic. You see, my mother was on the way to having an abortion. Yes, an abortion! As I write this, my emotions are running so deep to think that you would not be holding this book in your hands if that procedure was successful in terminating this resilient young African American Sailor of 35 years. Who would ever think that I am here today, and you are reading my book, because my dear mother heard the voice of God say – DON'T DO IT! I'm so glad that my mother didn't have that abortion. At the time of my birth, they never married. Eventually, they both went their separate ways, and my mother, a single parent at the time was left to raise a child during the turbulent years of the 1960's. Although my mother initially dropped out of high school, she ended up getting her high school diploma some 42 years later with the help and encouragement of the child that was almost aborted.

My mother's family did not have much education and, during the pregnancy my mother's mother was unemployed leaving no financial means of financial support for a grandchild. Much of the money earned was through farming, and housekeeping. However, through hard times, the family stayed in church.

On the other hand, while my mother was pregnant with me, the biological father had the benefit of all types of scholarship offers from colleges throughout the United States. You see, he was a very popular guy on campus. However, my mother was very concerned about the pregnancy of this new life that was to be with her for the next 18 years. The biological father and his family made it clear that they wanted nothing to do with my pregnant mother and the unborn child. There was no party to celebrate the life of this unplanned baby. For years, the biological father had no thoughts about the well-being of his "invisible" child.

In response to my mother's pregnancy, the father eventually encouraged my mother to have an abortion. Abortion was the only option that could have made the situation right. Fortunately, God spoke to my mother at the time. My mother heard the voice of God speaking to her in a way that was very audible. I remember my mother stating that "God didn't want me to have an abortion." However, at one point, my mother had tried to self-induce the abortion, but somehow, it didn't work. Just as the scriptures reminded me in Jeremiah 1:5 "Before I formed you in the womb, I knew you, before you were born, I set you apart, I appointed you as a prophet to the nation." OMG! God knew me, and no abortion could stop me from showing up on planet earth. I honestly believe that my life was destined at birth.

Realizing the uncertainty of the future, my maternal great grandmother, Mother Deans, the spiritual backbone of the family, was the focal point of my life. My mother told my great grandmother how painful it was for her, a teenage mother to suffer such humiliation without knowing what to do. My mother had the increasing sense that unless she forgave the biological father, a hard lump of revenge would be passed on to her unborn child. So, for months, my mother prayed and talked to God.

When I turned three years old, my mother met a man named James W. Barnes, who immediately fell in love with my mother, and they later moved to Washington, D.C. It was in the Nation's Capital that things began to really change. It was in the District of Columbia where I was raised in the housing projects and learned how to survive in an environment of crime, drugs and shooting. This is when I started to teach the neighborhood kids despite the conditions. However, my parents made sure we were protected.

In June of 1980, I graduated from high school. After high school, I continued to participate in evangelistic outreach projects and made several trips to and from North Carolina, and D.C., where I was exposed to a wider array of opportunities in ministry.

In April of 1983, after going from college to college and being uncertain about the exact course of study, I decided to join the United States Navy. Joining the military proved to be something different and it provided further training in leadership. Of course, there was not much in terms of good job security without an education. Moving back to North

Carolina did not seem very satisfying. There was nothing but lots of factories. Although I did not find factory work too appealing, I joined the Navy as an E1 (enlisted man), with no guaranteed "A" school. The next 14 years would prove to be a journey that would bring me to my ultimate calling as a Navy Chaplain that would become the genesis for a resilient road.

Upon completing basic training in Great Lakes, IL, I received orders to my first command, the USS PAUL (FF-1080) in Mayport, Florida as an un-designated seaman recruit. My first thought was; how did I get into this situation? Once you make a commitment as joining the military, all sorts of crazy and bizarre thoughts cross your mind. All I knew at the time was that I made this decision, now I had to make the best of it. I spent the next four years on board the ship, USS PAUL, and eventually struck out of deck department without ever attending "A" school.

As a former Navy Radioman first class (E6), my religious beliefs helped me succeed in my military career. After spending 15 years of active-duty service as an enlisted person, perseverance, being resilient and "keeping the faith" toward the road of a military officer, especially as a Chaplain, I finally reached my goal. In May of 1998, I was commissioned as an ensign in the Navy, Chaplain Candidate Program Officer (CCPO).

I always wanted to become an officer. Many influences on this life journey nurtured my way to fulfilling this lifelong dream. Although I did not have a complete understanding of the journey in my earlier years, God prepared a faith community of evangelistic-minded people that reached out of their comfort zones to instill values.

Prior to entering active duty, I was a minister. I remember giving my trail sermon at my Dad's store front church in Wilson, North Carolina. Additionally, before my commission, it took determination and a very long time to find my calling of fulfilling the position of a Chaplain. After missing the opportunity to participate in several career development programs, I kept the faith and vision to excel.

During my career, rejection letters came from Broadened Opportunity for Officer Selection ("BOOST"), and I even failed to select for Chief Petty Offer (E7). I also received a rejection letter from the Officer Candidate School ("OCS"). To make matters worse, I also was denied a request to participate in the Enlisted Commissioning Program ("ECP").

However, in 1995 while on active duty as an enlisted person, I earned a Bachelor of Science degree in Workforce Education and Development from Southern Illinois University, headquartered in Carbondale, Illinois. While stationed at Naval Training Center San Diego, California, I was an instructor teaching at the school that I was not qualified to attend due to low ASVAB scores. Additionally, I completed my Master of Arts degree one year after undergraduate education (while on active duty) from United States International University, located in San Diego, Ca.

In April 1989, I briefly departed the Navy and remained employed at the Pentagon as a government civilian information systems specialist (GS7). However, I realized that the civilian world was not the right fit and I missed the leadership challenges that the Navy provided.

In September 1989, I rejoined the Navy. After attending a Navy Veteran indoctrination course in Orlando, Florida, and was giving orders to the staff of Amphibious Group One based in Okinawa, Japan. After a two-year tour in Japan, orders were received to the staff of Commander Carrier Group One (CCG-1) based in Coronado, CA. After that tour, orders was received to the Naval Training Center, San Diego, CA. It was this duty station that I was an instructor at the very school that I could not attend, upon my initial job as a striker in the field. The center was closed as a result of the Base Realignment and Closure ("BRAC").

I enjoyed my instructor duty tour. As a resilient Sailor, leadership continued to be at the forefront for me. After instructor duty, new orders transferred me to the USS DENVER (LPD-9). While aboard USS Denver, I received my true calling ---- to spread the gospel! I held to my faith and took a bold leap of faith. A formal request was put in for an "early out" to apply for the Chaplain Candidate Program Officer Program

("CCPO"). It was then that I realized that ministry existed for me in the United States Navy.

After spending nine months aboard USS Denver, I departed the Navy with no severance pay, retirement income or a secure job. I left with nothing. An entire career was put on the line.

"You're crazy!" are just a few of the words that I received from fellow shipmates when they heard that I had made the decision to depart the Navy after 15 years of service. I made a request to speak with the Denver's Commanding Officer. Having a proven track record of being involved in the community, working with the ship's Chaplain and reaching out gave me the full support of my chain of command. Part of my responsibility was to motivate Sailors to become active in various community service projects and a myriad of other events.

Concerned about the education of children, I organized a group of Denver Sailors into participating in the annual Reading is Fundamental ("RIF") campaign in Balboa Park. The team passed out books to local elementary students to help sharpen their reading skills. Showing how these students could become resilient was key.

I received the backing of Denver's Commanding Officer. My request for "Early Out" was approved and I was wished well with my spiritual endeavor. In September 1997, I departed the Navy as an enlisted person for the final time. In 1998, my faith blossomed. My commission and ensign shoulder boards were received. Getting a commission was a dream come true.

I credit my positive upbringing and moral character training from my mother, father, great grandmother, and the community of local church families that were planted.

From birth, I was almost aborted and rejected from career programs in the Navy. Although the pain was unbearable, God allowed me to find hope and hang on a little longer. Just as God spoke to my teenage mother in an unplanned birth, God also spoke to my heartbroken soul and told me to not give up! However, for the first time in my life, faith was more than "silver and gold."

After completing Seminary, I received orders to my new duty station as a Chaplain. This was both rewarding and exciting. However, before departing on a six-month cruise, I and my then-wife had a discussion where we shared words, hurts, and struggles. After the deployment, I looked forward to returning home full of ministry stories, spiritually uplifted, and somewhat ambivalent, but knew that something was unsettled. Later that evening, I learned that my marriage was over.

To this day, I am unaware of how I drove around all night crying without driving off a cliff or into the nearest river (especially in Virginia Beach). Feeling abandoned and rejected without having a soul to talk to, all I could state was "Why was this happening to me?"

My pain was the type that morphine could not cure. For the next 6-12 months, I experienced hell and torment. I had lost everything! All of the money I had saved up on my six months' deployment was spend on attorney fees. I was preparing to reside in a shelter. There were no best friends to turn too and talk with me. Now, I could identity with the verse in Job: "Though he slay me, yet will I hope in him; I will surely defend my ways to his face."

I continued to smile, counsel and do the job knowing that inside my inner chambers, bitterness resided. To this day, I am forever grateful for godly parents who did not judge me. Both parents allowed me to cry and have a place to reflect during my rocky road dealing with life's experiences. I am Resilient today because of the love and understanding from God almighty and loving parents.

Crazy Faith

"Now faith is the substance of things hoped for, the evidence of things not seen."

Hebrew 11:1 (KJV).

The odds of you being born are 400 trillion to one. Many of us have been blessed with this knowledge, but few come close enough to experience it. A woman I know was pregnant with her first potential child. I say potential child because it was shortly after conception, and his birth was being debated in her head. As someone in an unstable relationship with a jock, the girl had to decide whether she should take on the responsibility of being a mother or abort the baby.

She decided to abort and was en route to the abortion clinic when a strong voice stopped her. She felt a voice speak to her in a manner ears can't pick up. It spoke through her and transformed her priorities. She knew in her mind that she would be freer if she went through with the abortion, but in her heart, there was something that wouldn't let her sign-off on the logic. She became so thoroughly convinced that abortion was not an option that those around her started saying she's crazy.

Have you ever had so much faith in something so against the grain that people have no option but to call you crazy? Well, if you stick with your position long enough, the world has no choice but to bend to your will. And that's what this young woman did.

She went through with the pregnancy. She stood by it in the first trimester; her boyfriend said she was crazy. She stood by it in the second trimester. Her boyfriend's parents said she was crazy. She stood by it in the third trimester, and everyone except a select-few thought she was crazy. And then, she gave birth and named her child Carl.

Yes, that child is me. I know the woman because she is my mother, and after the gift of life, the second most important gift she gave me was the gift of crazy faith. I have taken on life's challenges with determination and heart, overcome rejections, and pursued my dreams without reason because I have her kind of faith, crazy faith. And how could I not?

I am the product of crazy faith, and that's why it is the only type of faith I choose to have. Most books have introductions that fluff up the page-count, but as you can sense, I'm delivering you value right off the bat. I'm using the introduction space to convey the importance of having crazy faith.

"With an Attitude of Gratitude"

Your Treasure in My Story

"Be faithful in small things because it is in them that your strength lies" ~Mother Teresa~

From this, you must recognize that faith and knowledge are different things. People fail to leverage faith for their own good because they judge it on the metrics of knowledge. Yes, your knowledge has to make sense by the world's standards, but your faith is more valuable when it is unreasonable. You don't have faith in gravity; you have the knowledge of it. That's because it is very logical. Even when you can't see it, it doesn't qualify as a faith-based assumption because it is too reasonable. But when you believe having a child while being-resource strapped is somehow going to lead to good things, that is faith. In your life, when you need to have faith to get things done, discard the metrics of external approval, logic, and experience. Have crazy faith.

This memoir is more than just stories about my life. I believe a story is only as valuable as the lessons in it. And the stories enclosed in these pages help you build resilience. I only include the most powerful narratives from my life serving in the United States Navy, being a Chaplain, holding professional responsibilities, and becoming one of the top consultants in my space. I genuinely believe that there are treasures for you in stories of mine. And each chapter will include actionable advice. I hope its contents are as valuable for you as they have been for over one hundred thousand Sailors.

Your Treasure From Your Story:

_____

_____

_____

_____

_____

_____

_____

_____

_____

Attitude of Gratitude

"Giving thanks always for all things unto God and the Father in the name of our Lord Jesus Christ"

Ephesians 5:20 (KVJ).

Humans have knowledge of their own mortality. What they do with this knowledge becomes their legacy. I understood that I must cherish the time I had with my great grand-mother. So I'd sit with her and hold conversations long enough to be podcasts before podcasts were invented. And surprisingly, I did little talking as my great grandmother dug into her treasure trove of memories and told me stories from her life.

It is easy to miss your opportunity for education when you take your elders for granted. I learned many things from these true stories. She would tell me about saving up to buy her house during the great depression, about raising her kids, and how things used to be.

One day, I was sitting with her, listening to one of her stories, when something clicked. Suddenly, these were no longer disconnected stories joined by only the protagonist: my great grandmother. I started to notice a theme running consistently through each story. It was a feeling similar to having a blindfold removed.

I noticed that in each story, there were two things in common:
- She had it worse than me
- She was more grateful than I.

When you put it that way, you understand why she lived to play with her great-grand kids. I soaked up her perspective but couldn't organize it into a system of priority. I've always been grateful even for my challenges. But I only got the words to describe it when I joined the United States Navy.

One of my mentor Chaplains used to bring up the "attitude of gratitude." The first time I heard it, it sent shivers down my spine. As if he put a truth, I always knew in words I never had. "attitude of gratitude" became such a core perspective that I incorporated it into my signature. I'd still sign messages, emails, and even written letters with an "attitude of gratitude" footer.

Writing your truth is not just a way to communicate with someone else. It also helps you communicate with yourself. Today, the attitude of gratitude makes up the foundation of my resilience framework. But this wasn't always the case. I was often advice-bullied for being humble. Advice-bullying is when someone pushes upon you; advice he/she thinks is best for you while ignoring your ability to decide for yourself.

I was "advised" to stop being humble. Repeatedly told that I was too humble for my own good, I was about to re-think my position when an admiral said the right words at the right time: Humility isn't a weakness, it's a strength. Again, that bypassed my ears and spoke to my heart. He put a truth I had always known into words for me. And to this day, I'm grateful for all I have been, all that I was kept from being, and all I'll ever be.

"With an Attitude of Gratitude"

Your Treasure in My Story

"Develop an attitude of gratitude, and give thanks for everything that happens to you, knowing that every step forward is a step towards achieving something bigger and better than your current situation."
~Brian Tracy~

Cultivate an attitude of gratitude by focusing on what you're hungry for and realizing that you can only get there by being thankful for what you already have. An attitude of gratitude makes you count your blessings, and only by knowing how you're blessed do you know what you can use to get ahead. A man blessed by a ladder can't use it if he's too busy being discontent about not having two ladders.

Your Treasure From Your Story:

_____

_____

_____

_____

_____

_____

_____

_____

_____

_____

_____

_____

_____

_____

Listening

"Behold, I stand at the door, and knock: if any man hear my voice, and open the door, I will come in to him, and will sup with him, and he with me."

Rev 3:20 (KJV).

It might be odd to include listening as a step in becoming more resilient, but when you pay attention to the right voices, you become more steadfast in your beliefs. Going back to my original story, I would like to highlight that my mother listened to the voice that asked her to quit the trip to the abortion clinic instead of quitting the pregnancy. Had she listened to her doubts regarding the future, you would not be reading this book. It makes me emotional, internalizing the possibility of my mission never taking root in the material realm had she not listened to the right voice. My personal belief is that I not only exist because of that voice but exist for it.

As a Chaplain, I relied on listening to voices that belong to prominent people above and below in the chain of command to guide Sailors in the right direction, be it metaphysically or in their careers. And in doing so, I learned that the measure of a man's character is the voice he chooses to listen to.

Most of us jump to speaking because we have a fear of becoming invisible. We believe if we don't say something about everything, the world will ignore us. I, thankfully, never had to unlearn this habit. I've always been the curious kind and am grateful to have listened to the right people most of my life. But had I continued listening to my father; I would not have been in the Navy. All the lives I touched in the service would've gone without feeling my presence, but at a certain point, I chose to listen to my heart and the voice that speaks to it. I joined the Navy against my father's wish, and he became my biggest cheerleader.

As our parents' children, we don't understand that they're trying to figure out life as much as us. And while they take risks for us like my dear mother, who stood by me and faced the possibility of single motherhood and permanent poverty, they stop us from taking risks for our own lives. This is a natural result of having a heightened sense of protectiveness.

Listening doesn't mean blindly accepting. Listening doesn't mean immediately reacting. Listening means absorbing and reflecting. When I rose to a directorial position and had the responsibility of assigning Chaplains all over the world, I signed up for the drama associated with making people move to places they didn't want to go.

Things would often get heated, and I could have done a lot of damage, but Abraham Lincoln stopped me. Lincoln came up with an exercise that people learned about through his biographer. For decades people taught each other this exercise, and it kept passing down generations and demographics till it reached my RP, the gentleman who wrote my orders. And he passed it onto me.

I was mostly on speaker phone and he could see emotions run high, how could they? After all, assignments almost always involved uprooting people's lives and making them travel to different places. My Religious Program Specialist(RP) asked me to write the email I intended to write but to take twenty-four hours before pressing "send." I know you might be thinking, 'how Abraham Lincoln did his email exercise before the internet?' The man wrote letters when he was angry then took time to reflect before sending them. He never sent the letters, and a stack of them was found posthumously.

Now here's the twist: I did not know this was an exercise Abraham Lincoln performed. Even the Chaplain didn't know who was to be credited with the exercise. Had I chosen not to listen to his words just because he was junior to me, I would have rejected the wisdom of Abraham Lincoln.

"With an Attitude of Gratitude"

Your Treasure in My Story

"There is something in every one of you that waits and listens for the sound of the genuine in yourself. It is the true guide you will ever have.   And if you cannot hear it,   you will all of your life spend your days on the ends of strings that somebody else pulls."
~Howard Thurman~

Please do not make your listening contingent on whether someone is senior to you, a friend of yours, or has more money than you. And when you listen, make sure you're not skipping to rejection or accepting without reflecting. Listening to the right voices will pay dividends for decades.

Your Treasure From Your Story:

_____

_____

Perseverance

"But he that shall endure unto the end, the same shall be saved."

Matthew 24:13 (KJV).

Resilience and perseverance can often be confused because the terms are used interchangeably. I believe there's a subtle yet essential difference. I'm resilient; that's my character. I persevere; that's what I do. Therefore perseverance is a building block of resilience. And you should be glad for every opportunity to persevere because you get to build resilience. In short, perseverance is the workout, and resilience is the perfect body you want.

When I was trying to get a job at the Capitol Hill Hospital, I was rejected for four months straight. Rejection doesn't feel nice. We're built to take rejection personally. And when we get rejected, we can get caught up in questioning ourselves regarding our worth and what it all means. Interestingly enough, the young Carl Barnes was too hungry to get bogged down in the emotional drama.

Unlike my older self, I just kept going after my goal with no pause and consideration of context. As a result, I got hired as a dietary aide at the hospital. I did that job the best I could until they were short of cooks and got me in the kitchen. And got in the kitchen, I did. I learned to cook and out-cooked the cooks around me. And that's the result of perseverance.

Now let's flash-forward to another time in my life where I had the luxury of pausing and asking myself what the rejection meant. This was when 06' results were coming out. One of my friends asked me if I had seen the results. Having uncertainty about the results, I should have made it a point to locate them. He asked me to get off the phone and emailed me the list. When I went through the list, I couldn't find my name.

This crushed me in a way I couldn't acknowledge. I had an internal monologue regarding self-worth. Why wasn't I selected? Was I good enough? I knew the people who made it. I had decades of service under my belt. I had momentum behind me, yet I could not get the Captain rank (06). I knew it was inside me, but something kept it from becoming a reality.

Carrying all that weight and frustration, I wore a smile on my face. Every time I was happy for someone making it, the pain of me not making it would bubble up. This went on for a while until I was sitting across a civilian supervisor's desk. He looked at me and asked, "Barnes, are you okay?"

I broke down. I let it all out. It did not feel good to be rejected. But upon putting it out there, I realize it was only so painful because I had attached my self-worth to it. And that's where I paused and reflected. I remembered where I started from, and my attitude of gratitude returned to the forefront of my perspective. I dared to say to myself what I never thought I would: "Barnes, you started as a seaman recruit. You've come a long way. You didn't become a Captain (06). So what?"

"With an Attitude of Gratitude"

Your Treasure in My Story

"Success is not final, failure is not fatal: it is the courage to continue that counts"
~Winston Churchill~

I did not want to be the person who tells you to persevere by advising you to persevere. There is nothing actionable about that type of advice. I didn't even paint myself as a bastion of perseverance and cited two stories: one where I did persevere and the other where I became content with my position. The lesson for you is that your perseverance is directly attached to your hunger. The thing you are the most hungry for is the one you'll stay persistent in the pursuit of. Pick your goal, and be hungry for it. Most importantly, stay hungry and never pause to judge yourself because of a rejection.

Your Treasure From Your Story:

_____

_____

_____

_____

_____

_____

_____

_____

_____

_____

Asking For Help

"Ask, and it shall be given you; seek, and ye shall find; knock, and it shall be opened unto you:"

Matthew 7:7 (KJV).

We started out in caves and have built skyscrapers, yet the number one way of receiving help remains unchanged. If you want help, you have to ask for it. Let's talk about asking for help in a different light, though.

I've never been shy about asking for help. When I'd get in trouble with my mom, I would try to get my great grandmother to bail me out. And had I gotten in trouble with her, I'm sure I would have gone up in the chain of command and enlisted my great grandmother's help. From those days being a young child to when I was Chaplain Religious Enrichment Development Operations Director (CREDO) in the US Navy, I have always been open to receiving help. However, I got better at receiving help.

We all take help from those "above us," in rank, seniority, and resources. And that's what I did as a child because the only people junior to me were infants who could do nothing but cry. But when I was Chaplain Religious Enrichment Development Operations Director (CREDO), people, supposedly my juniors, were better-versed than me in certain things. I had my juniors coaching me. I even asked them for advice on technology, "Yes, I am your supervisor, but I don't know this specific thing, so please help me." I would say.

At other times in my life, help came without asking. I remember I had my surgery, and my movement was strictly limited. My nephew looked at me and said, "Uncle, you're on the floor; you might as well pray." I could have reacted based on the fact that he's my nephew. "How dare you ask me to pray," I could have said. But I took the kid's advice and prayed.

At other times you will find yourself in need of help, and no one will be willing to offer it. My divorce was one of the most impactful things in my life. I didn't ask for it; it was handed to me. And in my community, I had to live as if I had demanded it. As far as people were concerned, I was a divorced Chaplain. The ones who wished to dismiss me didn't care for my role in the whole thing. They didn't care about the lengths I went to in order to avoid this from happening.

I was painfully aware of what this could mean to my audience. Remember that my entire existence was aimed at being an impactful Chaplain. I was born a survivor with credit going to no one but God and my mother, who listened to him. Spreading his word was always my sole goal, and here I was in a situation that was hurting the human side of me with love lost and also my mission.

When I sought support, people prioritized their opinions of divorce over my well-being. And that's when I learned to turn to the one who helps unconditionally at all times in all situations: God. I went to God, and I asked him to refill my internal wells. I asked him to top off my ability to persevere. I asked him to refill me with a momentum-building appetite. I asked him to heal the wounds on my heart and self-esteem. And he came through.

"With an Attitude of Gratitude"

Your Treasure in My Story

"A person is not defeated by their opponents but by themselves."

~Jan Christian Smuts~

Remember to ask for help and be open to receive it. You may receive help when you don't ask for it or ask for help and not receive it. Either way, it doesn't hurt to ask, but it can hurt to expect. The other 'person' you can expect help from is God. Ask for his help every day to make your day better. And if every coming day is better than the one before it, life's good.

Your Treasure

From Your

Story:

_____

_____

_____

_____

_____

_____

_____

_____

_____

Self-Care

"Casting all your care upon him; for he careth for you."

II Peter 5:7 (KJV).

When working as a Radioman "A" instructor in San Diego, I was so preoccupied with providing value for most of my pupils that I forgot to take care of my most important student: myself. I still remember how it became routine for me to work all day and use my car as my bed at times. One day, I commuted back from a night class and fell asleep in the car only to wake up in the hospital because I was burned out. This, of course, was earlier in my career, and I have come to realize the importance of self-care towards the end.

When I got the responsibilities of being a CREDO director, I had the pleasure to plan retreats, and I've incorporated them into my lifestyle since. If you're reading this book, you're very likely to be the type of person with a strong drive and an aim for accomplishment.

This chapter isn't about my brilliance, but the thought that haunts me when I look at all my degrees, certificates, medals, and honors. I see in all of them the opportunities I missed—the ones for taking a pause, relaxing and giving myself credit. I'm still very grateful for having learned my lesson when I did. Self-care is essential to resilience.

But I wasn't always the guy who would single-handedly plan a self-care getaway for his birthday to take in the Washington DC Christmas vibe. I wasn't always the man who stays at cozy Bed and Breakfast places and treats himself when he needs to recharge.

My desire to serve clouded my judgment, and I refused to say "no" for most of my career. I took on responsibilities I didn't have to in some instances. I still remember traveling to DC on my own dime because I wanted to be on active duty and go before the care board because there was no funding. "You're not going to reject me; I want this, I'll get this." I still remember the words echoing in my head. I sacrificed 15 years for this. But as much as I was supposed to push through that time, I was also supposed to take a pause and exhale after it.

Self-care is not slacking on your responsibilities. Imagine you're driving a car from Minnesota to California. If, throughout your journey, you're so single-minded about reaching Cali that you don't even stop at a gas station, how far do you think you'll make it? Life is a lot like the drive from Minnesota to California; you need many rest stops. That is normal, and we have to normalize self-care so we can be more resilient.

I love to talk to people about their passions and desires. A lady once told me about her desire to feel the sands of Hawaii under her toes. You'd not think that a story of fulfilling one's desire could get slightly tragic. But she said, "Barnes, I wanted to retire and relax in Hawaii, but only a few months before I could get there, I had a stroke. Now I get to feel the sand on my toes while I'm in a wheelchair."

"With an Attitude of Gratitude"

Your Treasure in My Story

"It's one of the most beautiful compensations of this life that no man can sincerely try to help another without helping himself."
~Ralph Waldo Emerson~

Please remember that when you're on your deathbed, you'll not ask for more time to work. It is good to have a servant's heart, but you cannot go very far if you don't take care of yourself. Please be mindful of your body's cues of exhaustion and burnout. There is no nobility in being tyrannical to yourself. Plan retreats and provide yourself the care you deserve.

*Your
Treasure
From Your
Story:*

_____

_____

_____

_____

_____

_____

_____

_____

_____

_____

Having the Right Mindset

"Let this mind be on you, which was also in Christ Jesus."

Philippians 2:5 (KJV).

Do you ever think back on what you said you were going to do and went through with doing? For me, One such moment was witnessing the stage all being set as a graduation ceremony was being prepared, and recipients would walk the stage at United States International University, now Allient University, in San Diego, CA. I can still remember an emotion bubble up in me till it expanded into the burning desire that possessed me. I could not wait to speak it into existence. Positive affirmations came out of my mouth: "Next year, I am walking that stage." Keep in mind that this was in no way "practical" by the world of the university standards.

Then I did something different. Many people say bold things, but few dare to stand by them. I stood by my words when the University said they couldn't let me graduate on that time line. When I said, I had to get it next year because my goal was to have my 1st Masters before I had to deploy the following year. Yes, I was to deploy the following year. Guess what? They came back with a schedule that allowed me to take extra hours. Sure enough, when the next year's ceremony came around, one of the Masters recipients was none other than yours truly.

Pay attention to the words you say because they're the amplification mechanism for your mindset. People who think negatively say negative things and consume their own words to become more negative. This happens for positive people as well, albeit with positivity. If you wish to be resilient, you have to have the right mindset in every area.

Remember that despite rising through the ranks in the United State Navy and getting four-star Admirals and Generals to pen recommendations for me, I never made Chief Petty Officer (E7). I wasn't a test-taker. But that didn't stop me from cheering for all my friends who made it. I will not lie, it hurt to feel left out, but life will bring disappointments; you have to pick your battles. My goal to spread the right words to the people who need them the most wasn't tied to my rank in the Navy. So I picked what I prioritized.

I still remember being involved in a book Launch of a former student who became a best-seller in four categories overnight. And her words warmed my heart. She said in front of everyone, "You thought so much of me that I dared to think I could do this. And here I am."

Sometimes, people only need to witness that belief to make the extraordinary happen. If my belief in her could make this happen, imagine what my belief in myself could do. And I can look at my trophies and honors and credit the people who instilled the right mindset in me. The Les Browns, Antonio T. Smith, Jrs and John Maxwells of the world helped me believe in myself. They made me learn that with the right plan and resilience, a child almost aborted then dismissed to a life of poverty could actually rise above what the world dismissed him to.

It makes me emotional, even thinking about how much impact the right mindset has made in my life. Over one hundred thousand lives are positively impacted because I chose to speak the right words in existence over a 35 year military career give or take a few.

"With an Attitude of Gratitude"

Your Treasure in My Story

"I read myself out of poverty long before I worked myself out of poverty."
~Walter Anderson~

Therefore, your mindset is not a responsibility you have towards yourself but also towards those around you. A great mindset will make you happier and more resilient. More importantly, it will pay dividends in uplifting those around you.

Your Treasure From

Your Story:

_____

_____

_____

_____

_____

_____

_____

_____

_____

_____

_____

_____

_____

_____

Change Your Circle

"Don't fool yourselves.
Bad friends will destroy you."

1 Corinthians 15:33 (CEV).

You do certain things that matter so much, yet you're unable to see their importance. In my godson, David's life, our trips to the Redskins' stadium was such an inspiration. I often took him there, and we would look at the skyscrapers and the buildings being built around the stadium. Flash forward to a time we reconnected later in life.

As I stepped out of the airport to be welcomed by the elements, I found David with a warm smile and confidence in his gait. I had to pay for nothing; he took care of me from that point for the whole trip. "Mr. Barnes, I want to show you something," he said as he drove to a high rise. DEG Construction said the sign.

"What's this?" I asked. "That's David E. Gorham's Construction company. My company. Remember how you used to take me to the stadium and I saw all those skyscrapers? Now I build them. Thank you." I realized then that merely exposing him to the right environment and letting him dream that big was the best gift I could give him.

As I teared up with joy over David's success, I had flashbacks of the people who connected me to opportunities and those who blocked my path. People who said "you're crazy" when I dreamed big and those who said "you aren't crazy enough" to push me forward.

I returned from that visit with a renewed mindset. I had to let go of the "friends" who were not aspiring to raise their vibe. It is challenging to acquire friends on higher levels, but you can do it if you're determined.

At one of my lowest points, going through a divorce, my circle was so full of judgmental people that I had to take on the additional burden of self-judgment when love lost was already hurting my heart. Only my parents were supportive. My refuge was working out by waking up before the sun came out. It got me busy. Do you realize how lonely one has to be to take shelter in exercise? I was that person. Forget not that I was still a Chaplain with a happy face and many people physically around me, at least during the daytime. But real loneliness is not having the right circle.

Today, when I look around, I see high-level connections like coaches certified by John Maxwell, others with partnerships to Les Brown and Antonio T. Smith, Jr. These people would never judge me. They encourage me, educate me, and inspire me. This isn't a circle I was given. It was the one I chose. What's your choice?

"With an Attitude of Gratitude"

Your Treasure in My Story

"You are the average of the five people you spend the most time with."
~Jim Rohn~

Get intentional about your social circle. Most friendships are formed due to the convenience of geography or proximity. Some even boil down to shared interests. But what you must keep senior to all of this is whether the friend you acquire is an asset or a liability. You must be assets to each other to have a mutually beneficial friendship. Resilience is a game that requires cheerleaders at certain times. Make sure you have an abundance of cheerleaders

Your
Treasure
From Your
Story:

_____

_____

_____

_____

_____

_____

_____

_____

_____

_____

_____

_____

_____

Reading

"Study to shew thyself approved unto God, a workman that needeth not to be ashamed, rightly dividing the word of truth."

II Timothy 2:15 (KJV)

One of the first books I read was Who Moved my Cheese? And It is all about dealing with movement in one's work life and living environment. Later on, I found myself drawing from that well as the Deputy Detailer assigning others to different places. One day I was sitting at my desk after helping a fellow Chaplain understand how he can deal with his assignment and what it entails for his life. I thought about the principles I communicated regarding movement and dealing with a new life. And the words echoed in my head, "Who Moved my Cheese?" I smiled.

Then I blocked some time out to think about every book, the title of which would come to my mind. We read lots of books, but if any book has ideas that take hold, we remember their titles at least vaguely. From The Hood to the Hill: A Story of Overcoming. It is written by Dr. Barry Black, a Chaplain who I look up to. He became the first African American USN Chief of Chaplain and now the 62nd Chaplain of the United States Senate, Rear Admiral (Ret.), U. S. Navy. I remembered how the story describes his life with his mom in the projects. She gave him money to memorize scripture. That little shift changed the trajectory of his life.

Another book that came to mind during this session was Intentional Living by John Maxwell. I've also read almost every book by Les Brown. Do you know the common thread among all of these? The fact that each of these books ended up transforming lives.

Who Moved my Cheese made me good at helping Chaplains deal with sudden movement in assignments and, consequently, their lives. I read Les Brown and am now connected to one of his prodigies, Antonio T. Smith, Jr. I read John Maxwell and am now a John Maxwell certified life coach. Finally, I read books that weren't even self-help, but they took me to places all over the world. In my US Navy career, I've traveled to almost every country I've read about. This has brought me to the firm conclusion that books are a way to control your destiny, along with reading the Bible.

"With an Attitude of Gratitude"

Your Treasure in My Story

"We have an innate desire to endlessly learn, grow, and develop. We want to become more than what we already are. Once we yield to this inclination for continuous and never-ending improvement, we lead a life of endless accomplishments and satisfaction."
~Chuck Gallozzi~

Books help you open your mind. They take your mind to places you want it to go. And remember that wherever your mind goes, your body goes as well. Just like every book I read became a part of my life's journey, the ones you read will define where you go. To be resilient, you must have the assets to keep going when everyone else will give up. Get very selective about the books you read while simultaneously increasing the number of books you consume. If you aren't a reader, I recommend you get an audible.com subscription and consume your favorites in the audio book form.

Your Treasure From Your Story:

Face Your Darkness

"I will not be afraid of ten thousand of people, that have set themselves against me round about."

Psalms 3:6 (KJV).

I have just returned from the funeral of a comrade. It was an emotional affair. He received Veteran of Foreign Wars (VFW) honors, and seeing the tribute and witnessing the casket draped in the flag touched my heart in ways I cannot put to paper. They talked about his legacy and how he came back against all odds, did multiple tours in Vietnam, and received a purple heart.

This made me think of my legacy. I remembered hearing that one's legacy is that small dash between his birth date and his death date. What we leave behind is the service we provide. For the same reason, this book isn't so much about my stories but about the value you can get from reading them. You can see how much I value your time and prioritize giving value because both the introduction and the epilogue are packed with actionable lessons.

As I reminisce about the brave soul that has passed on, I can't help but wonder if he knew he was that loved. Did he know how much his peers admired him? I sure hope that he accepted himself, loved himself, and admired himself as much as we all did.

"With an Attitude of Gratitude"

Your Treasure in My Story

"We come this way but once. We can either tiptoe through life and hope that we get to death without being too badly bruised or we can live a full, complete life achieving our goals and realizing our wildest dreams."
~Bob Proctor ~

Accept the person in the mirror. You may not be perfect, but you are you. Cultivating the right circle and being of service will bring about a great tribute at your funeral, but you won't be there for it. So live with your own approval because in its absence, no one's approval matters.

Understand that you have tremendous potential as well as an incredible destructive potential. Whichever side of you gets fed is the side that wins. Accept yourself with all your flaws and stop wishing circumstances were different. You are dealt a hand in life. Your responsibility is to play it the best you can.

Your fears, base emotions, and mistakes can create a villain you may ignore too long. Acknowledge the things about yourself that need to be fixed. You will realize that in doing so, you develop crazy faith in yourself, invite gratitude into your attitude, start listening actively, and persevering where required. If you understand your personality's shortcomings, you can ask for help, indulge in remedying self-care, and produce the right mindset. Most importantly, facing your dark side means choosing the right circle of friends, so they feed your positive side and reading the books that chase away the darkness. As a consequence, you become resilient enough to be practically rejection-proof.

Your Treasure From Your Story:

_____

_____

_____

_____

_____

_____

_____

_____

_____

_____

_____

_____

_____

_____

_____

_____

_____

_____

_____

_____

_____

Dedication

I'd like to dedicate this book to my parents
Rev. JAMES W. BARNES and
Evangelist MINNIE R. BARNES.

ATTITUDE OF GRATITUDE

"Honor your father and your mother, so that you may live long in the land
the Lord your God is giving you…"
Exodus 20:12 (NIV).

Dr. Carl M. Barnes

"What Is Life"

Life is like an onion,
You must peel it one layer at a time.
And sometimes you cry.
Life is challenging; meet it.
Life is a gift; accept it.
Life I a sorrow; overcome it.
Life is a tragedy; face it.
Life is a duty; perform it.
Life is a game; play it.
Life is a mystery; unfold it.
Life is a song; sing it.
Life is an opportunity; take it.
Life is a journey, complete it.
Life is a promise; fulfill it.
Life is a beauty; praise it.
Life is a struggle; fight it.
Life is a goal; achieve it.
Life is a puzzle; solve it.
You are powerful.
Develop self.
Work on yourself.
You are worth all your effort.
The keys to you motivation are to
Know that you have something to give.

~Anonymous

"With an Attitude of Gratitude"

"You are not defeated until you quit."

~Antonio T. Smith, Jr

There were so many of you who purchased books that I was unable to keep up with writing a personal letter to each of you.

With this page, I want to thank each and every one of you for purchasing this book and thank you for pushing through and living the resilient life style!

Each of you are absolutely wonderful. Please accept this gift of my gratitude for your love and support.

"With an Attitude of Gratitude"

~Dr. Carl M. Barnes

About The Author

A retired military officer, Carl tells the inspiring story of almost being aborted by an abandoned and fearful teenage mother, his steadfast resilience in overcoming insurmountable odds, challenges and setbacks driven by his low ASVAB SCORES, and his multiple disappointments over 35 years in the military as he attempted to climb in the ranks. His remarkable success story in spite of the odds, from enlisted man (E1) all the way to Commander (05), and the many incredible points between, is a story readers will learn from and gain tremendous insights for their own challenges.

Dr. Carl M. Barnes' personal decorations include 5 Meritorious Service Medals, 3 Navy and Marine Corps Commendation Medals and 5 Navy Achievement Medals. He is also the recipient for the Military Outstanding Volunteer Service Medal. He was also nominated for the 1994 President's Volunteer Action Award and The Golden Rule Award. He is a recipient of "Keepers of the Dreamer" Award in 2015. He is the recipient of the Big Brother of the year award, and Silver Spoon award. Listed in Who's Who among students in American Universities & Colleges.

Dr. Carl M. Barnes has a Bachelor of Arts in Workforce Education and Development from Southern Illinois University. Dr. Barnes has a Master of Arts in Education from the United States International University of San Diego, a Master of Divinity from Bethel Seminary and a Master of Science in Counseling and Psychology from Troy University. Dr. Carl M. Barnes studied at United Theological Seminary where he received a Doctor of Ministry.

Dr. Carl M. Barnes is the author of: 21Day Devotional Nuggets For Resilient Living, The Bounce Back Effect: How to Soar in The Midst of Setbacks and co-author of 5 Strategies of Resilient Living: How To Turn

Pain Into Purpose. He is also the CEO and Founder of CALL ME BIG BROTHER(CMBB), INC, a 501(c)3 nonprofit.

Carl is a sought-after international speaker with a story of Resilience and Hope, who lives in Memphis, TN and enjoys being a life-long learner, cooking, spending quality time with his immediate family and creating a lasting mark on the world *"With An Attitude of Gratitude"*.

www.ingramcontent.com/pod-product-compliance
Lightning Source LLC
Chambersburg PA
CBHW031437120626
46545CB00006B/2449